# The Memo

By Teresa Marie Banks
and Family

Illustrated by Teresa Rudd

The first day of summer was finally here.

Ryan and Andrea gave out a big cheer!

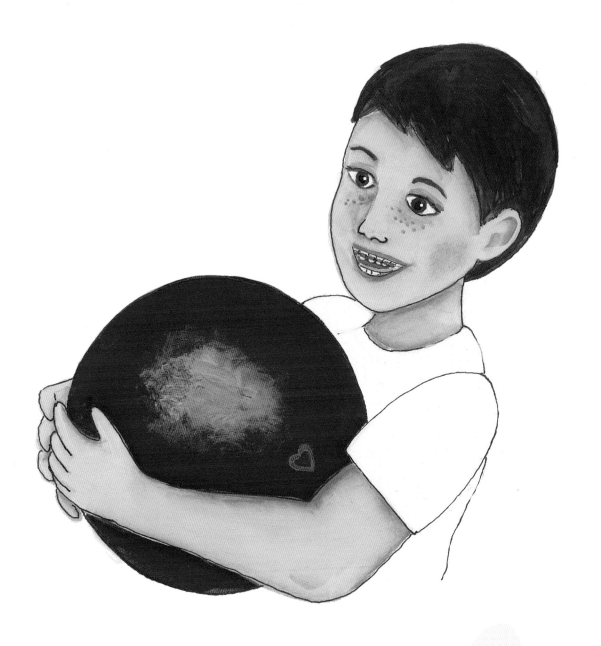

There was so much to do; but where to begin?
Ryan found a red ball and showed a big grin.

The kids kicked the ball through the squishy brown mud, until it crashed through the window with a thud.

On their white shirts they
wiped the dirty brown mess.

**Some New Adventure Waited For Them,
Can You Guess?**

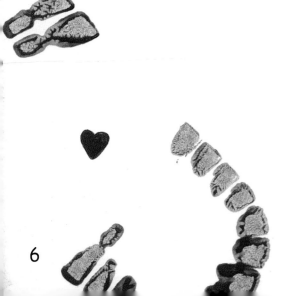

The warm morning sun made them tired and hot.
Something icy cold would really hit the spot.
Music from the ice cream truck was barely heard.
And off the kids ran without speaking a word.

They chose orange popsicles
to eat on the lawn.

And slowly they licked them
until they were gone.

On their white shirts they wiped
the sticky orange mess.

**Some New Adventure Waited For
Them, Can You Guess?**

There was time before lunch to find more to do.
They rode down a steep hill and away they flew.

A bump in the road brought them both to the ground.
Bodies and bike grease were splattered all around.

Ryan and Andrea were covered in grime.

They headed for home.

They had run out of time.

On their white shirts they wiped the greasy gray mess.

**Some New Adventure Waited For Them,**
**Can You Guess?**

They swiftly ran home to consume a big lunch.
Anything Mom prepared would be good to munch.

15

Spaghetti was ready when they reached the door.
They quickly ate it all and still wanted more.

The kids noisily ate and finished the food.
They hurriedly left and tried not to be rude.

On their white shirts
they wiped the spaghetti red mess.

**Some New Adventure
Waited For Them,
Can You Guess?**

From outside they heard
the familiar dog bark.
Grabbing the leash,
they headed for the park.

The enormous black dog was friendly and fast.
Ryan and Andrea ran hard not to be last.

Winning the race by not letting the dog pass,
the kids took turns wrestling him in the grass.

19

On their white shirts
they wiped the grassy green mess.

**Some New Adventure Waited For Them,
Can You Guess?**

As Ryan and Andrea played,
time quickly whirled by,
they grew hungrier
and hungrier
and let out
a big sigh.

Some bubblegum ice cream would taste good to eat.
So off they went to ask Mom for a cold treat.

They ate the ice cream
as slow as they could.

Every last drop tasted,
oh so very, very, good.

On their white shirts
they wiped the bubblegum blue mess.

**Were There More Adventures
For The Day, Can You Guess?**

Evening had arrived and they had to head home.
Slowly they walked, there was no more time to roam.

The day went by quickly with all they had done.
They were sad it ended, it was so much fun.

24

Ryan and Andrea were feeling so blue.
They looked down at their shirts and
suddenly knew.

The memories of the day
would always be there.

Shown in the colors
of their daily affair.

Their stained shirts told the stories of their play.

Can you remember their adventures that day?

# Reading-the Foundation of Your Child's Education

Read to your child every single day – especially at night before bedtime. Establish this habit as part of your child's daily routine. This sets the quiet tone needed for your child to settle down and fall asleep.

Interaction while reading books needs to be adjusted for each child's attention span and age level. Some children need to be engaged with pictures and asked "What's that?" Other children can just listen to all the words and will memorize the story as it is read over and over again.

Sit close to your child, touching and cuddling him/her or all of your children. Use vocal inflections and expression as you read. Answer their questions. Let your children talk about each page. You can ask various questions as well:

- What will happen next?

- Where is the _____?

- Who will _____?

- Who is this?

- Why did _____ happen?

You can, also, have your child find various things on the pages. That is why the gratitude hearts are hidden or just in plain sight to be found. Hearts and hands on the Memory Shirt can be counted. Colors of the hands can be found and named.

The most important concept is: "Books are fun". Reading is something that will be with our child for a life-time. Books are a way to show your love.